THREE BROMSGROVE POETS

Geoffrey Hill
Molly Holden
A.E. Housman

Introductions by Alan Holden
Compiled and illustrated by
Robin Shaw

The Housman Society

First published in 2003 by
The Housman Society, 80 New Road, Bromsgrove,
Worcestershire, B60 2LA
This second edition published 2012

Designed by Robin Shaw
and typeset by Jennie McGregor-Smith
In Palatino Linotype, mainly 9.5 point

Printed in Great Britain by Henry Ling Limited, Dorchester

Compilation and editorial text © The Housman Society

Poems of Geoffrey Hill © Geoffrey Hill

Poems of Molly Holden © Nicola Carpenter and Gerard Holden

Illustrations © Robin Shaw

All rights reserved. Without limiting the rights under copyright reserved, no part of this publication may be reproduced, stored in or introduced into a retrieval system or transmitted in any form or by any means (electronic, mechanical, photocopying, recording or otherwise), without the prior permission of both the copyright owner and the above publisher of this book

ISBN 978-0-904579-22-2

THREE BROMSGROVE POETS

Second Edition
with additional poems
by
Geoffrey Hill

HOUSMAN SOCIETY PUBLICATIONS

The Westerly Wanderer by Jeremy Bourne (1996)
Biography of A.E. Housman, ISBN 978-0-904579-06-2

Housman's Places by Robin Shaw (1995)
Places important in the life of A.E. Housman,
ISBN 978-0-904579-03-1

Unkind to Unicorns ed. Archie Burnett (1999)
A selection of Housman's comic verse, ISBN 978-0-904579-16-1

A.E. Housman Poet and Scholar - Westminster Abbey 1996, (1996)
The Testimonials which led to A.E. Housman's acceptance into
Poets' Corner, ISBN 978-0-904579-08-6

Soldier, I wish you well ed. Jeremy Bourne (2002)
The military poems of A.E. Housman and the letters from
Burma of his brother Herbert, ISBN 978-0-904579-13-0

Inseparable Siblings by Elizabeth Oakley (2009)
A portrait of Clemence and Laurence Housman.
Published by the Housman Society through Brewin Books,
ISBN 978-1-85858-440-9

Housman and Heine - A neglected relationship
ed. Jeremy Bourne (2011)   ISBN 978-0-904579-21-5

Available from bookshops and The Housman Society,
18 College Road, Bromsgrove, Worcestershire B60 2NE

CONTENTS

Foreword and Acknowledgments	7
GEOFFREY HILL	9
From *Mercian Hymns*:	
I, XIV, XXI, XXII, XXV	15
From *Tenebrae*:	
An Apology for the Revival of Christian Architecture in England,	
13, The Herefordshire Carol	20
From *Canaan*:	
Sorrel	20
Pisgah	21
Mysticism and Democracy, Part One	22
Of Constancy and Measure	23
From *The Triumph of Love*:	
VII, LIII, LXXXII, CVII, CXXXVII	24
From *The Orchards of Syon*:	
extracts from XXII, XXXVIII, XLVIII and LIV, LV in full	27
From *A Treatise of Civil Power*	31
A Cloud in Aquila	
MOLLY HOLDEN	33
Dodderhill Woods	37
Teens	38
Worcestershire Lanes	39
Button Oak to Arley	40
Photograph of Haymaker, 1890	41

Housman Country		42
New-born		44
Generations		44
Of 1959		45
Illness		46
Birthplace		47
After the Requested Cremation		48

A.E. HOUSMAN   49

From *A Shropshire Lad*:

II	Loveliest of trees, the cherry now	53
XXVII	Is my team ploughing	54
XXIII	The lads in their hundreds to Ludlow come in for the fair	56
XXXI	On Wenlock Edge the wood's in trouble	57
XXXII	From far, from eve and morning	58
XXXV	On the idle hill of summer	59
XL	Into my heart an air that kills	60
LII	Far in a western brookland	61

From *Last Poems*:

XXXIX	When summer's end is nighing	62

From *More Poems*:

XXIII	Crossing alone the nighted ferry	64
XXXI	Because I liked you better	65
XLVII	O thou that from thy mansion	66

From *Additional Poems*:

IX	When the bells justle in the tower	66

For details of publication of Geoffrey Hill's and Molly Holden's poems see page 68

FOREWORD AND ACKNOWLEDGMENTS

In this anthology The Housman Society celebrates three poets who were all profoundly influenced by Bromsgrove, its setting in Worcestershire, its proximity to Severnside, the borderland beyond and the ancient history of the midlands.

In 1896 Alfred Edward Housman was putting together the collection of poems he had recently written. Living in Highgate, and now Professor of Latin at University College London, he recalled his early life and the countryside he had enjoyed as a boy living in Perry Hall and at the Clock House; the fairs, the farms, the spires – his 'happy highways' — and the views to the west that had inspired him — his 'blue remembered hills'.

In the 1960s and 1970s Molly Holden, living close to St. John's church, was bringing up a family. Stricken by illness, her urge to enjoy the countryside and write poetry was only heightened. Worcestershire was a substitute for her beloved Wiltshire, but she embraced it and wrote perceptively about it. Sadly she died in 1981.

Geoffrey Hill has been writing since the 1950s and , his poems continue to draw on his Bromsgrove origins — his 'Goldengrove'.

Housman is widely read and appreciated after all this time but is well worth rediscovering. Molly Holden's published works are all out of print, and many poems are yet unpublished. They deserve better. And although Geoffrey Hill is considered to be among the finest of contemporary poets there must be many who have not yet enjoyed his works.

In this second edition we continue to thank Geoffrey Hill for personally making this selection from his poems and especially for the two extra poems which are so relevant to Bromsgrove. We also thank his publishers, Penguin Books, for allowing us to print them.

Alan Holden died in 2007. For the first edition he selected his wife's poems and wrote the introductions to all three poets. I was grateful to him and am grateful to his son, Gerard Holden and daughter, Nicola Carpenter, who are the copyright holders for Molly Holden's poems, for permission to reprint them.

The poems by A. E. Housman are now out of copyright but for the first edition this lay with The Society of Authors. I thanked them then and remain grateful to them for their generosity to The Housman Society.

Finally our thanks are due to Jennie McGregor-Smith for preparing the typescript for printing.

Robin Shaw

GEOFFREY HILL

Geoffrey Hill, spoken of by many critics as the best living English poet, was born, the son of a policeman, in Bromsgrove in 1932 and was brought up in Fairfield. His family roots, on both sides, have been in Worcestershire, and in the Bromsgrove area especially, for at least the last 200 years. His paternal great-grandfather was a blacksmith at Shrawley, near Stourport; his mother's family, 150 years ago, were nailers living on Staple Hill, Lickey End. He was educated at Bromsgrove County High School, which was subsequently incorporated into the comprehensive system as North Bromsgrove High School. As we shall see in his poetry, he was deeply influenced by his surroundings, and although he has lived in the United States for some years his poetry still harks back to his roots.

From Bromsgrove he went on to take a first class degree in English Language and Literature at Keble College, Oxford, and thereafter followed a distinguished academic career. He lectured for many years at the University of Leeds before being appointed as Lecturer in English at Emmanuel College, Cambridge. He went on to be Professor of Literature and Religion at Boston University in Massachusetts. He is also Honorary Fellow of Keble College, Honorary Fellow of Emmanuel College, Fellow of the Royal Society of Literature, and Fellow of the American Academy of Arts and Sciences.

For this book Geoffrey Hill has made his own choice of poems from the volumes *Mercian Hymns* (1971), *Tenebrae* (1978), *Canaan* (1996), *The Triumph of Love* (1999), and *The Orchards of*

Syon (2002). As will be observed, all the poems contain references to Bromsgrove, Worcestershire, Herefordshire, and nearby places; a number of these references, especially in the later poems, include material concerning his own life.

In a note on *Mercian Hymns*, the poet refers to the historical King Offa, who reigned in the years AD 757-796, but points out that Offa in these poems 'might be regarded as the presiding genius of the West Midlands'. The form of the poems, taken — according to Geoffrey Hill's note — from Latin canticles of the early Christian Church, carries admirably the fusion of the historical and the modern which makes for fascinating effects.

The poems taken from *Canaan* and the other two later books are separated from *Mercian Hymns* by twenty-five years. A reviewer once wrote that 'Everything in Hill's style … relates to his visionary purpose'. One of the epigraphs in *The Orchards of Syon* may help the reader to understand this 'visionary purpose'. 'Everything was at rest, free, and immortal' is taken from one of Thomas Traherne's *Centuries of Meditations*. Traherne, a seventeenth-century writer of poetry and prose of a rare beauty and luminousness, is part of the English visionary tradition in literature and art which includes Vaughan, Blake, Samuel Palmer, Edward Calvert and D.H. Lawrence, though Vaughan was born in Wales and his landscape is predominantly Welsh. For these men, the natural world, especially the English landscape, offers visual beauty and also glimpses into another, more shadowy, less tangible world, a kind of lost paradise; for several of these artists, the vision is a religious one and often associated with childhood. This is so in Traherne's *Third Century*, where the corn was 'Orient and Immortal Wheat' the young men 'Glittering and Sparkling Angels', and so on.

For Geoffrey Hill, these glimpses are less pure, more troubled and problematic. In a number of his poems, the terrifying modern world of war and cruelty obtrudes, to be grappled with in dense and powerful language, though there is no suggestion that earlier history shows us a less violent and a more cheering world. ' Of Constancy and Measure' from *Canaan* is written in memory of the poet and composer Ivor Gurney, who suffered grievously as an infantryman in the trenches of the western front in the Great War and had several periods in mental institutions after the war, until his death in 1937. He was sustained in his torments by memories of his beloved Severn and the Gloucestershire countryside, as, increasingly, Geoffrey Hill has turned in later years to 'Goldengrove', or Bromsgrove. From the same volume, 'Pisgah' (the Old Testament mountain from which the Promised Land could be seen and the name given by the Housman children to the hill opposite their Fockbury home) appears to be a memory of his father in the garden of the poet's boyhood. Here the language is clearer and less difficult than is sometimes the case, sharp in its sense of movement and light – the 'flitter of sweet peas', the 'incandescent aura' of blossom.

This same sense of the here-and-now set against an elusive otherwise is found in the first section of the extract from 'Mysticism and Democracy': the 'polished desk surface' as the poet writes, which is part of the 'darkling mirrors /to an occult terrain'. But the second part offers the reader only an occasional physical glimpse into a more abstract world in which he gropes for solidity.

The selections from *The Triumph of Love* contain numerous references to the locality – Romsley, Fairfield, Stourport, Lickey and others. Kenelm, the martyr remembered in the dedication of Romsley church, is referred to in ways similar to the Offa of *Mercian Hymns*, at once historical and modern. But the local and the personal can slide into the visionary, as in No. LIII, where the boyhood memory at the beginning is left for the 'all-gathering English light', where each bead of drizzle 'at its own thorn-tip stands/as revelation' — an exact observation which perhaps glancingly suggests Christ wearing the crown of thorns. In No. VII, the water tower on the top of Romsley Hill, a symbol of everyday, peaceful life, changes into the mast of a warship, which bombards Coventry before that city was laid waste by bombing during World War II. In No. CVII, the *Flos campi* (lit. 'flower of the field', a phrase found in the Old Testament Song of Solomon) is both the flower which grows on disused railway-lines and the Vaughan Williams music, which suggests a tranquil world, unsuited to the 'disnatured century'.

The 'Syon' in the title of Hill's latest book is more often found nowadays as Zion. Hill's title recalls the medieval English book of mystical devotion, *The Orcherd of Syon*. These, then, are the orchards near the Heavenly City. In this book the natural world of England, the world of dream or vision (there are several references to the Spanish playwright Calderon's *La vida es sueño* — Life is a dream), the world of Hill's boyhood, and glimpses of something beyond earthly existence melt into each other or clash. Thus in the first extract, from No. XXII, the Clock House and Valley Farm, part of Housman's world, show the poet 'en rêve for Goldengrove'. This name for Bromsgrove is presumably taken from Gerard Manley Hopkins' poem 'Spring and Fall: to a young child' of which the opening lines are

> Margaret, are you grieving
> Over Goldengrove unleaving?

and the last lines

> It is the blight man was born for,
> It is Margaret you mourn for.

In No. XXXVIII, the child and the grown man are both present, but the struggle for consolation and belief is shown in the lines near the end —

>   I
> wish greatly to believe: that Bromsgrove
> was, and is, Goldengrove; that the Orchards
> of Syon stand as I once glimpsed them.

This poet is too honest to give himself, or us, false comfort: the breaking of the sentences over the lines shows the effort.

The same surprising uses of language as are found throughout Hill's work are found in abundance in this volume — at the end of No. XLVIII, St John's church 'gloaming' on the hill, the sandstone 'like mouldered plaster' of No. LIV and so on. The brooding No. LV is more difficult to follow. Yet even here the imagery is locally rooted. It seems to refer near the beginning to the struggle between the search for truth and sincerity and desire for art, artifice. There is a reference to the fallibility of memory — 'The eye /elaborates its tears' is in fact a deliberate misquotation of something quoted in No. LIV — an important point, given the many uses in the whole book of remembered details from earlier years, where the love of nature and the otherworldliness of Christianity are sometimes aligned, sometimes not.

As will be obvious, Geoffrey Hill's poetry requires close and attentive reading. Even then, the reader may not be completely sure of his or her whereabouts; but the effort will have been amply rewarded.

Alan Holden, 2003

Geoffrey Hill is currently Professor of Poetry at Oxford University. We have included in this edition two additional poems by him which are of special significance to Bromsgrove.

Mercian Hymns XXV is the poet's tribute to his grandmother, who was one of the many nailers who worked in cottage forges around Bromsgrove. Their story is tragic. At the end of the nineteenth century the coming of machine-made nails was making it impossible for the nailers to earn a living. In this poem 'darg' is an archaic dialect word for a day's work and 'Fors Clavigera' is the title of a series of letters written by John Ruskin, dedicated to British workmen, expressing his social vision.

A Cloud in Aquila explores the fate of Alan Turing who is now recognised not just for his vital role in code breaking at Bletchley Park but as a key founder of computer technology. After the war Turing was charged with homosexuality under existing legislation. He died of cyanide poisoning. The official verdict was suicide. The Bromsgrove connection came about when Turing at Sherborne School formed an intense friendship with Christopher Morcom whose family lived at the Clock House – that same Clock House where Housman had spent his formative years. It was close to the small hill which the Housman children called Mount Pisgah, (see pages 11, 21, 51, and 62). Christopher Morcom died while still at school and Alan Turing subsequently paid several visits to the Clock House, sharing his grief with Mrs Morcom.

Robin Shaw, 2012

MERCIAN HYMNS I

King of the perennial holly-groves, the riven sandstone:
    overlord of the M5: architect of the historic rampart and
    ditch, the citadel at Tamworth, the summer hermitage
    in Holy Cross: guardian of the Welsh Bridge and the
    Iron Bridge: contractor to the desirable new estates:
    saltmaster: money-changer: commissioner for oaths:
    martyrologist; the friend of Charlemagne.

'I liked that' said Offa, 'sing it again.'

MERCIAN HYMNS XIV

Dismissing reports and men, he put pressure on the wax,
    blistered it to a crest. He threatened malefactors with
    ash from his noon cigar.

When the sky cleared above Malvern, he lingered in his
    orchard; by the quiet hammer-pond. Trout-fry
    simmered there, translucent, as though forming the
    water's underskin. He had a care for natural minutiae.
    What his gaze touched was his tenderness. Woodlice
    sat pellet-like in the cracked bark and a snail sugared
    its new stone.

At dinner, he relished the mockery of drinking his family's
    health. He did this whenever it suited him, which was
    not often.

MERCIAN HYMNS XXI

Cohorts of charabancs fanfared Offa's province and his
    concern, negotiating the by-ways from Teme to Trent.
    Their windshields dripped butterflies. Stranded on
    hilltops they signalled with plumes of steam. Twilight
    menaced the land. The young women wept and
    surrendered.

Still, everyone was cheerful, heedless in such days: at summer
    weekends dipping into valleys beyond Mercia's dyke.
    Tea was enjoyed, by lakesides where all might fancy
    carillons of real Camelot vibrating through the silent
    water.

Gradually, during the years, deciduous velvet peeled from
    evergreen albums and during the years more treasures
    were mislaid: the harp-shaped brooches, the nuggets of
    fool's gold.

MERCIAN HYMNS XXII

We ran across the meadow scabbed with cow-dung, past the
    crab-apple trees and camouflaged nissen hut. It was
    curfew-time for our war-band.

At home the curtains were drawn. The wireless boomed
    its commands. I loved the battle-anthems and the
    gregarious news.

Then, in the earthy shelter, warmed by a blue-glassed
    storm-lantern, I huddled with stories of dragon-tailed
    airships and warriors who took wing immortal as
    phantoms.

MERCIAN HYMNS XXV

Brooding on the eightieth letter of *Fors Clavigera*, I speak this in memory of my grandmother, whose childhood and prime womanhood were spent in the nailer's darg.

The nailshop stood back of the cottage, by the fold. It reeked stale mineral sweat. Sparks had furred its low roof. In dawn-light the troughed water floated a damson-bloom of dust –

not to be shaken by the posthumous clamour. It is one thing to celebrate the 'quick forge', another to cradle a face hare-lipped by the searing wire.

Brooding on the eightieth letter of *Fors Clavigera*, I speak this in memory of my grandmother, whose childhood and prime womanhood were spent in the nailer's darg.

From TENEBRAE : AN APOLOGY FOR THE
REVIVAL OF CHRISTIAN ARCHITECTURE IN
ENGLAND

13 THE HEREFORDSHIRE CAROL

So to celebrate that kingdom: it grows
greener in winter, essence of the year;
the apple-branches musty with green fur.
In the viridian darkness of its yews

it is an enclave of perpetual vows
broken in time. Its truth shows disrepair,
disfigured shrines, their stones of gossamer,
Old Moore's astrology, all hallows,

the squire's effigy bewigged with frost,
and hobnails cracking puddles before dawn.
In grange and cottage girls rise from their beds

by candlelight and mend their ruined braids.
Touched by the cry of the iconoclast,
how the rose-window blossoms with the sun!

From CANAAN

SORREL

*Very common and widely distributed . . . It is called
Sorrow . . . in some parts of Worcestershire.*

Memory worsening – let it go as rain
streams on half-visible clatter of the wind
       lapsing and rising,

that clouds the pond's green mistletoe of spawn,
seeps among nettlebeds and rust-brown sorrel,
perpetual ivy burrowed by weak light,
makes carved shapes crumble: the ill-weathering stone
salvation's troth-plight, plumed, of the elect.

PISGAH

I am ashamed and grieve, having seen you then,
those many times, as now
                       you turn to speak
with someone standing deeper in the shade;
or fork a row, or pace to the top end
where the steep garden overlooks the house;
around you the cane loggias, tent-poles, trellises,
the flitter of sweet peas caught in their strings,
the scarlet runners, blossom that seems to burn
an incandescent aura towards evening.
This half-puzzled, awkward surprise is yours;
you cannot hear me or quite make me out.
Formalities preserve us:
                       perhaps I too am a shade.

From MYSTICISM AND DEMOCRACY

Part One

Ill-conceived, ill-ordained, heart's rhetoric:
hour into hour the iron nib hardly
                        pausing at the well –
inscribed silver, facets of Stourbridge glass,
polished desk surface; the darkling mirrors
                    to an occult terrain:
mystical democracy, ill-gotten, ill-bestowed,
as if, long since, we had cheated them,
                            our rightful, righteous
masters, as though they would pay us back
                                terrific freedoms –
Severn at the flood, streaked pools that are called
                                      flashes
wind-beaten to a louring shine.

OF CONSTANCY AND MEASURE

i. m. Ivor Gurney

One sees again how it goes:
rubble ploughed in and salted
                            the bloods
haphazard fatalities
our scattering selves allowed
their glimpse of restitution –
                            the orchards
of Sarras or Severn bare
plenitude first and last –
as if constancy were in time
given its own for keeping
                            as such gifts belong
to the unfailing burden of the planet
with so much else believed to be fire and air

THE TRIUMPH OF LOVE   VII

Romsley, of all places! – Spraddled ridge-
village sacred to the boy-martyr,
Kenelm, his mouth full of blood and toffee.
A stocky water tower built like the stump
of a super-dreadnought's foremast. It could have set
Coventry ablaze with pretend
broadsides, some years before that armoured
city suddenly went down, guns
firing, beneath the horizon; huge silent whumphs
of flame-shadow bronzing the nocturnal
cloud-base of her now legendary dust.

THE TRIUMPH OF LOVE   LIII

But leave it now, leave it; as you left
a washed-out day at Stourport or the Lickey,
improvised rainhats mulch for papier-mâché,
and the chips floating.
Leave it now, leave it; give it over
to that all-gathering general English light,
in which each separate bead
of drizzle at its own thorn-tip stands
as revelation.

THE TRIUMPH OF LOVE LXXXII

Go back to Romsley, pick up the pieces, becomes
a somewhat unhappy figure. I speak
deliberately like an old man who last saw it –
Romsley – through a spinning bike-wheel, as indeed
Kenelm may have done. That hook of ridge,
Waseley to Walton, was enemy country. Now
I overrun it in fiction. But Fairfield repels
my imperium, and always did. Its complex
anarchy of laws would have defeated Athelstan,
let alone Ine. High swine-pasture* it was,
long before Domesday; and will be again,
albeit briefly, at the flash of Judgement.
Let it now take for good a bad part of my
childself. I gather I was a real swine.

* Forfeld, the Anglo-Saxon name for Fairfield means 'swine-pasture'.

THE TRIUMPH OF LOVE CVII

Flos campi-time again among the small
ruins, vestiges, memorials, of the uprooted
midlands railways. How suggestive the odour
of hawthorn, building from the rubble
of craft and graft. What was it that growing
girls could get from *Virol*? Were boys forbidden it
for their green-sickness? Could it have fed
our mutually immature desires? How
English, how vivid, how inapposite
to the disnatured century: a slow, Lydian-mode
wayfaring theme for unaccompanied viola.

THE TRIUMPH OF LOVE CXXXVII

The glowering carnival: nightly solar-flare
from the Black Country; minatory beacons
of ironstone, sulphur. Then greying, east-northeast,
Lawrence's wasted pit-villages rising early,
spinning-wheel gear-iron girding above each
iron garth; old stanchions wet with field-dew.

THE ORCHARDS OF SYON
Extract from XXII

      Low-laid
at the dayspring: less self-renewing
censure; more mourning sickness. I was *en
rêve* for Goldengrove, which you had elegized
some generations since, untouched, beyond
the Clock House and the Valley Farm
in a different country. I recall
my thoughts as yours, and sounds, far more than thought,
the saw-mill's flintering squeal. Aeons
deepen their recession. To such ends
no-one's drawn gifted. Misrepresentation's
power play. With what fiction
should we defend our verdicts, retransmit
voices along the waveband?

THE ORCHARDS OF SYON
Extract from XXXVIII

Did we shield then, believe it, hope to die,
those all-marvelling, unrehearsed
hours, where goldcrests and the great ferns were,
Osmunda regalis, bowing us in and down,
both royal and nesh?   I am conversant with
the book of recollection, self-
desolating child, part-changeling.   Ancient
vows are unexempted,
in some way signify the natal language
not forgotten.   Intermittent
cloud-shadow across roofs.   Our loves discerned
like stars depth-hung in water.
Impassively the sempiternal casts
deep for endurance.
And here – and there too – I
wish greatly to believe: that Bromsgrove
was, and is, Goldengrove; that the Orchards
of Syon stand as I once glimpsed them.
But there we are: the heartland remains
heartless – that's the strange beauty of it.

THE ORCHARDS OF SYON
Extract from XLVIII

                   You need to weigh this
by constant reckoning. I am not the judge;
these are not directions. Never let
my voice mislead you. I may be mistaken;
self-mistaken; wrongly self-possessed;
confusing jealousy with righteousness
as I would have it
whatever wrongs we do, one to another;
our midlands far and wide; LAWRENCE, his
New Jerusalem *in the mind enthroned,*
time for bestowal, shadow into shadow,
St John the Baptist gloaming on its hill.

THE ORCHARDS OF SYON
Extract from LIV

    … , I desire you
to fathom what I mean. What dó I mean?
I think you are a muse or something,
though too early rejected. The dank
Triassic marl, sandstone like mouldering plaster,
can't all-inhold you. From Burcot to Worms Ash
the rock sweats and trickles, even in winter,
the sun digs silver out of the evergreen.
Orchards of Syon, tenebrous thresholds
of illumination, a Latin love
elegist would comprehend your being
a feature of his everlasting dark.

THE ORCHARDS OF SYON LV

I desire so not to deny desire's
intransigence. To you I stand
answerable. Correction: must once have stood.
What's this thing, like a clown's eyebrow-brush?
O my lady, it is the fool's confession,
weeping greasepaint, all paint and rhetoric.
Empower the muse; I'm tired. Shakespeare, who scarcely
brooded on perfection, perfect so many times.
Memory! memory! *The eye
elaborates its tears*, but misremembered,
misremembering no less key-clustered
mistletoe, the orchard's châtelaine.
I may well carry my three engraved thoughts
out beyond Shrawley whose broad verges once
throve like spare garden plots with pear and apple
or with wild damson, thinner on the ground.
O my lady, this is a fool's profession
and you may be dead, or with Alzheimer's,
or happily still adoring a different
Duke of Illyria. I have set you up,
I confess thát, so as not to stint
your voice of justice. Love grows in some
way closer to withdrawn theology.
The Deists' orb drops below Ankerdine.

From A TREATISE ON CIVIL POWER

A CLOUD IN AQUILA

1.
Get him out of there – Turing, out of
the *Turing Machine*. Some hope, if the rules
of immortality can be bent. I
should hope so.

2.
The world of his prediction is not ours
as he conceived it. If there is innocence
it was as here: phase, segment; region
of Aquila

3.
that validates and haunts first love, verifies
disappointment itself, *meaningless
in the absence of spirit*, whatever
the mechanism

4.
of the thing, desire, the singing calculus;
impossible pseudo-science, Eddington,
McTaggart: their measure of the mind
nubilate, precise,

5.
roving existence at call. Any way
the idea of love is what joins us thus far
though not past all question in the same
tissue of body;

6.
and Morcom is dead now and Turing with him;
the Clock House demolished. At the sharp turn
where it was always dark the road steepens
to Housman's Pisgah.

MOLLY HOLDEN

Molly Holden, my late wife, was born Molly Gilbert in London in September 1927. Her parents were middle-class; her paternal grandfather, Henry Gilbert, was a novelist and short-story writer whose work was mainly published in the late 1890s or the early 1900s; Molly later found herself fascinated by the same areas of study as her grandfather had followed, notably prehistory, archaeology and mythology, especially Celtic.

In Spring 1940 the family moved to Swindon. The Wiltshire countryside, with its downs, ancient trackways, hill-forts, tumuli, and great prehistoric monuments, in particular Avebury, became an absorbing interest for her; the poetry she was writing from about the age of ten, where natural presences were so powerful, began to take in this new world, which was, as she said, 'the country of my heart'.

In 1945 she began studying English at King's College, London. I met her in 1947, after I had returned from a three and a half year stint in the army to take up again the English course I had started in 1943. She took her degree in 1948, I in 1949, and in October 1949 we married and started on our M.A. degrees; this was then a two year full-time course, with a substantial thesis and examination papers. Her subject was the growth of interest in the antiquities and early history of Wessex as shown in English Literature; I edited some medieval manuscripts. We completed our M.A.s in 1951.

In 1952 I took up a teaching post in Stockton-on-Tees, and

we began to buy our first house. Our children, Nicola and Gerard, were born in 1953 and 1955 respectively. I moved to Bromsgrove County High School (now North Bromsgrove High School) in 1956, and Molly and the children moved to Bromsgrove in 1957, after I had managed to find a house to our liking. Here Molly stayed until her death in 1981: I still live in the same house.

When the children were young, Molly had almost no time for writing, but she turned again to poetry as time went on, and achieved some success in having poems accepted by local newspapers and the BBC Midlands Service. Our quiet and happy family life received a terrible blow, however, when in late 1962 she was diagnosed as having multiple sclerosis – her deterioration into becoming an invalid was quite rapid: by the end of 1964 she could no longer walk. She was 37, our children 11 and 9.

Much of her frustrated energy went into poetry. She had had a pamphlet, *A Hill Like a Horse*, privately published in 1963 with the aid of some money from an aunt, and another small collection, *The Bright Cloud*, published in 1964 by Outposts Publications. Poems now came in increasing numbers, and did so until near her death. Although family holidays soon became an impossibility, we were able, thanks to a legacy from a distant relative with which I bought a car in 1962, to go out on many occasions into the Worcestershire, Herefordshire, and Shropshire countryside which she came to love almost as much as her beloved Wiltshire. She would sit and observe places, people, wildlife, and landscapes with an intensity and accuracy which is reflected in the verse. Another room was built onto our house to compensate for the dining–room, now of necessity made into a downstairs bedroom; here she would sit, looking at trees, shrubs, flowers, birds, and changing skies and seasons. These formed what she called 'the solid food of a curious poetry'.

Her great reward came in 1968, when Cecil Day Lewis, Poet Laureate, and poetry editor for Chatto and Windus, accepted for publication her volume *To Make Me Grieve*, which came out in the latter part of the year to excellent reviews, especially in *The Times Literary Supplement*. A second book, *Air & Chill Earth*, was published by Chatto and Windus in 1971 and a third, *The Country Over*, in 1975. Invitations to send poems to numerous newspapers and journals followed, as well as interviews for BBC radio and the British Council. Between 1967 and 1973 she also wrote four novels for children, three of which were also published by Chatto and Windus.

At our family doctor's insistence, I arranged to take a slightly longer holiday than usual in 1981, whilst Molly went into the care of a local hospital. I was recalled urgently after only five days, as her condition had worsened. She died on 5 August. She was cremated, and I scattered her ashes on her beloved Liddington Hill, in the downs near Swindon.

Since her death, there has been one other volume, Carcanet's *New and Selected Poems* of 1987. Additionally, individual poems have been reprinted in numerous anthologies, and there have been occasional readings on BBC radio.

Molly's poetry is wide-ranging in subject matter. The landscapes and history of Wiltshire and the Marches, family life, children, adolescence, her illness and limited life, literature and painting – all of these and more are found in abundance, in over 600 poems, about 400 of which remain unpublished. Her style seems effortless and natural, but in fact much more skill and craft is employed than is obvious at first sight. She uses insistent alliteration (as was used in Anglo-Saxon poetry) in her poem 'Hastings' (not chosen here) as a tribute to the Anglo-Saxon world largely swept away by what she regarded, as many others still do, as the inferior culture of the Normans in 1066. 'Button Oak to Arley', a poem about a stretch of the Severn near Bewdley, is a skilfully constructed sonnet, consisting of two sentences, the second of ten lines leading with sure aim to the last lines, where the river comes into view. Or look at 'Dodderhill Woods', where the pain of no longer being able to walk in the woods in autumn emerges only in a throwaway 'I recall' in line 11. The first three stanzas contain half-rhymes only - 'fiery/airy', 'hell/feel', 'wildfire/were', and so on, but the poem is clinched by the only full rhyme – 'husk/dusk'.

But in truth it is the deep human insight, the sharp observation, and the often wry tone that holds our attention in what one reviewer summed up as 'precise lacerating poems'. Look at the way in which the last lines of 'Photograph of Haymaker, 1890' vividly brings present and past together – or rather there is no present and no past, only the timeless moment of the poet's vision; or the secret world of 'Teens'; or the fight for life in the baby Thomas Hardy in 'Birthplace', where the small room 'with its mysterious two-way look at life' captures the essence of the great writer's subtle, elusive insight. These are, in general, easily accessible poems, but should not be underestimated.

Alan Holden

DODDERHILL WOODS

This is my annual November pilgrimage,
to pass through an uncoloured afternoon
of grey air, cottages, grass, hedges half-blown,
and come upon the woods at the hill's edge

whose fallen leaves should promise nothing further.
But this we look for as we come – wildfire
among the sodden trees as if the sun were
setting low and warm. But that's not so, rather

the wet cold here is fiercer but brilliant-fiery
as in the icy flames of some old Irish hell.
And, I recall, to walk here is to feel
apparent embers underfoot as well as airy.

Only a few birds speak. A squirrel drops a husk.
The black of rain-soaked trunks is curious emphasis,
as if intentional, to that ignis fatuus
defying the known season and the seen dusk.

TEENS

That was always my place, preferably
    at dusk, in a slight rain
– below the drenched allotment bank,
    by the bridge not often shaken by a train.

The neat hedge ended there, the fields began,
    sloping to shrouded hills,
and the lane grew pot-holed, led only
    to flowery pastures and abandoned mills.

There I would stand in the mizzle, watching
    thirty martins or so
hawking silently above the meadows,
    high on black lines of flight, eerily low

as the heads of grasses, swerving
    only at a solid hedge
and me, a contentedly brooding phantom,
    at the lane's, at the night's, edge.

WORCESTERSHIRE LANES

This country differs from dry uplands, water hereabouts
is no white rarity. The muddy ditch
the Saxons named still moves beside the road
and milking-time soon churns the yard to sludge.

Men could build where they would; farms
five fields apart and cottages in threes up tracks
now detail slope and hollow, and lanes mizmaze
the countryside, hedges a screen for lover and for fox.

Thorn, hazel, briar, make them alike, easy
to lose one's way, different in small things only –
empty beehives in a gangling orchard, a church
with no apparent parish, shock-yewed and lonely.

Sometimes these lanes go by, irrelevant as thoughts,
for miles with only magpies, padlocked gate, and crop,
a philosophic pattern to the man born locally,
to others only metaphors without a map.

BUTTON OAK TO ARLEY

You would not think, on this quiet woodland track,
drama would be so near; but turn and take
the eastward lane that passes round the back
of that blue-painted cottage by the oak.
It keeps quite level for perhaps half a mile
then drops abruptly, its descent concealed
by its precipitation, alpine style,
between high hedge-bank, thorn, and barley field,

and comes on narrow meadows suddenly,
a wide fast stream, and wooded hills each side,
air thick with slanting birds, martin and swift,

– the River Severn shouldering steadily,
above the reach here of the highest tide,
secret and sensual in its oak-furred rift.

PHOTOGRAPH OF HAYMAKER, 1890

It is not so much the image of the man
that's moving – he pausing from his work
to whet his scythe, trousers tied
below the knee, white shirt lit by
another summer's sun, another century's –
as the sight of the grasses beyond
his last laid swathe, so living yet
upon the moment previous to death;
for as the man stooping straightened up
and bent again they died before his blade.

Sweet hay and gone some seventy years ago
and yet they stand before me in the sun,
stems damp still where their neighbours' fall
uncovered them, succulent and straight,
immediate with moon daises.

HOUSMAN COUNTRY

These Shropshire marches carry his name
for those who know him well although
he was no native of these parts. Shropshire
for him was the sight and then the memory
of blue-ridged hills in the West, on the horizon,
seen from the field above his home
in Worcestershire; but his own particular
equivocal nostalgia lurks about these lanes
and blends most easily with what must always be
an element of difference for Englishmen who
travel the other side of the Severn.

            How his thinking
still pervades this countryside! Unexpectedly
one afternoon, exploring high land not quite
hills north-east of Ludlow, we came upon
a village football match. A grey sky pressed
from Wenlock Edge to Bredon, goal posts
stood white against the mulberry hedge,

the pitch was summertime's rough grazing, just
the size. Boys with intent and rosy faces
and jerseys bright as paint dodged in the mud;
the lane was packed with unexpected cars
and men leaned shouting upon gateposts,
roofs, and bonnets, loud and uninhibited.
We did not stop, for all the gaiety – we were
so patently outsiders – but had to slow to pass
and saw it all in one quick eager stare.

Now, what was there about that scene to
set the mind upon mortality, and unrequited love,
and distances of man from man? Only his images,
his words, echoing in the memory to make
a microcosm of a mucky country game.

NEW-BORN

Skin sodden, genitals grotesque, the wail
of a demon, a withered face of fury
above a tiny knotted chest at odds with the world:
how love such a little animal?

but its indignation, its burning sense
of injustice! Where is warmth, dark,
pulses of sustenance? why have they gone?
It is pity that possesses one at first.

And then, peaceful for the moment at the breast,
see the promise of beauty, the downy skull
– a furnace to the cheek – the arctic blue
of eyeballs. It will become human yet.

GENERATIONS

No children see their parents in their prime
(the getting them was spice of that bright time);

so when another sixteen years have passed
and children turn enquiring eyes at last

upon familiar faces of their youth
they only see the middle-ageing truth.

They'll never know how long hair suited me,
how blond you were, how we walked amorously

down evening lanes in Somerset and Kent
(do they think hawthorn thickets were just meant

for present youth's philandering alone?)
Come now, they in their turn will moan

time's revolution, seeing their children's eyes
widen with that same disquieting surprise.

OF 1959

Pink dress, pink shoes, pearl earrings,
dark hair pleated and pinned, walking
under limes, accompanied by
a dark and dreamy child, a fair
and vivid one – so, as I was ten years ago,
I would be remembered. But will not.

We play less part than we would like
to think in our children's memories. Of
that day, if anything at all, they'll remember
only the scent of flowers, myself
a tall uncoloured presence. The loving woman
in the chair, of later years, is how
I'll stay, and their father stooped.
Unless, as they grow old themselves, faint
glimmerings return, of a dark young woman,
of a fair laughing man.

ILLNESS

Poetic justice is imperfectly exemplified in me
who, as a child, as a girl, was persuaded that
I felt as earth feels, the furrows in my flesh,

buttercups curdling from my shoulder blades,
was what I saw. The rain would fall as pertinent on me
as on the lichens on the flint-embedded wall.

I had always a skin too few, identified
with sun-hot blossom on the far side of the road,
felt beneath my own warm envelope of flesh

the foreign winter that calcined the delicate
bones of the organ-grinder's shuddering monkey.
A ploughed field poniarded my chest.

So now it seems a wry desert that youthful
ecstasies, my earthly husks of joy,
should be so turned about by this disease

that feels like mist upon my fingers, like
a cold wind for ever against my body, and
air and chill earth eternally about my bones.

BIRTHPLACE

Two small windows, south and north, light
this shallow cottage's central room
upstairs; afternoon's sunlight streaming in
at one from orchards, fields, cottages,
all comfortable things, leaves in the other,
looking through shadow, a cool green view
of distance, the lonely heath, absorbing woods.

In this room, most probably at night,
the midwife turned, the oil lamp flickering,
from the tired woman on the bed to
the child laid aside for dead and saw
the even fainter flicker yet of life.
Her rough hands found the breath
and helped him fight for it and so
must share to some extent, in this
small room with its mysterious two-way look
at life, the credit for our haunting
by Tess among the winter fields,
by Gabriel Oak watching Orion rise.

AFTER THE REQUESTED CREMATION

A steady north-north-west wind preferably,
though an east wind would do as second-best,
and so my bones' smoke and innocent ashes
would carry into Wessex or the west.

I'd like my dust to be deposited
in the dry ditches, among the fine grass of home,
on hills I've walked, in furrows I've watched making
in Wiltshire's chalk-bright loam.

If not that then Wolverhampton's chimneys
might send me Severnward; that would do instead.
Those rose-red farms, those orchards, have all been precious.
I'd like to fertilize them when I'm dead.

Make no mistake though, it'll not come to choosing.
There'll be a west wind in the week I go.
Or else my southern dust will fall on hated highways
and be for ever swirling to and fro.

Well, as I'll never know, it doesn't matter.
I'm not, in truth, romantic about death.
Only I'd like the right wind to be blowing
that takes the place of breath.

A.E. HOUSMAN

A.E. Housman was born in Fockbury, two miles from the centre of Bromsgrove. His birthplace, the Valley House, is now called Housmans. Housman's grandfather, the first vicar of Christ Church, Catshill, had married into the family that owned the Fockbury estate, which included the Clock House, a manor house of seventeenth century origin, since replaced by two modern houses. Housman's father, a solicitor, married and briefly occupied the Valley House before moving to Perry Hall, which survives as a hotel in Kidderminster Road. Here Housman and his six younger brothers and sisters grew up, until the death of their mother (when he was twelve) led to their father taking the family back to Fockbury to live in the Clock House.

Housman was educated at Bromsgrove School and St John's College, Oxford. He was a brilliant Latin and Greek scholar; it was therefore very surprising when he failed his final examinations at Oxford. For some years he performed humdrum tasks as a Civil Servant at the Patent Office in London; during this time he published numerous papers on classical subjects in learned journals, which enabled him to secure appointment as Professor of Latin at University College, London, in 1892. He became Kennedy Professor of Latin at Cambridge in 1922. During these years he became a scholar of international renown – and a famous poet.

Housman had always written poetry and humorous verse. It was in 1895/96, when he was living in Highgate, that he wrote most of the poems which were published in the latter year as *A Shropshire Lad*. He was at a low ebb. The failure at Oxford still weighed on him, and he was haunted – as was some of his poetry to be – by his unrequited love for a fellow-student at Oxford, Moses Jackson. *A Shropshire Lad* took a while to establish itself, but when it did, it was reprinted many times: new editions still appear. Housman published only one other book of poems in his lifetime, *Last Poems*, in 1922. Two collections were published after his death in 1936, *More Poems* and *Additional Poems*.

We offer here a small selection of Housman's poems drawn from the four books. Many of the poems do not have titles, and are identified by the initials of the titles of the books (*ASL* and so on) and Roman numerals. This poetry, which draws deeply on English rural life and scenery, is also evidence of the writer's profound knowledge of Greek, Latin and English Literature. The result, however, is not poetry simply for the informed; it expresses strong emotions articulated through generally simple language and in formal stanzas.

ASL XXXIII ('From far, from eve and morning') is a good example of his skilled use of language   Here all but a few words are single syllables and all but two words are from Old English. Housman understood, and wrote, Latin as easily and skilfully as he wrote English; yet he chose, for this haunting poem, to use a vocabulary which everyone can understand. The mystery of human life – what brings us with our manifold characters, desires and dreams, into existence and then after a while fragments this unity into disparate parts – has seldom been better caught.

Similarly *LP* XXXIX ('When summer's end is nighing') expresses exquisitely the heartache which is latent in the end of summer and the beginning of autumn. The day and the season are coming to an end – as is the life of the speaker; night and darkness are near, and the hope that underlies much of human life ebbs with the light. The hesitancy and melancholy are underlined by the unusual five-line stanza which catches the reader unawares. Another aspect of this poem is that it is clearly autobiographical and suggests why Housman made Shropshire the setting of his poems. When he was in his teens, Housman would often go to the top of the small hill near the Clock House (the one that now carries a television mast), and watch the sun go down. To the west there are distant views of the Clee Hills in Shropshire - Arcady was there.

Soldiering and death in war always moved Housman. In *ASL* XXXV ('On the idle hill of summer') the worlds of dream, of death, and the love of comrades coincide, as the natural world ('the flow of streams') and the intrusive military world ('the steady drummer') coalesce rather than collide. This poem shows Housman's sense of poetic structure as the speaker, like one in a trance, rises to follow the path of glory, which leads to death. Such poems perhaps explain the appeal of Housman's work to soldiers on active service in both world wars.

Much more could be written of Housman's exquisite language. Essentials in any anthology are *ASL* II, ('Loveliest of trees') and *ASL* XL, ('Into my heart an air that kills'). These are probably Housman's best known poems and perfect examples of his skill.

In *MP* XXXI ('Because I liked you better') and XXIII ('Crossing alone the nighted ferry') Housman poignantly suggests how he suppressed his feelings for Moses Jackson. *ASL* XXIII ('The lads in their hundreds to Ludlow come in for the fair') shows how Housman may have transposed his experience of Bromsgrove rural life into Shropshire. It creates a picture of the throng at a rural fair such as Housman would have known from his childhood in Perry Hall, very close to the site of the Bromsgrove fairs that were held on Watt Close. *ASL* LII ('Far in a western brookland') is possibly more autobiographical than might seem today. In A.E.H.'s days Bromsgrove was a town of mills and mill pools, many of which are now gone – one was the huge Cotton Pool behind Perry Hall.

Concluding our selection, and demonstrating again the perfection of Housman's language, is *AP* IX ('When the bells justle in the tower'). Has there ever been a more concentrated four lines, with such sheer force? The key words – 'justle' (with its sense of hurried, impatient and urgent movement), 'hollow' and 'sour' – are emphasised and there is a strange appositeness in the parallel between the external noise and the internal soul-sickness. In the end though, what matters here, as in the other poems, is not anything which we may hesitantly try to say about them, but the immediacy and the impact of the lines on the reader.

Alan Holden

A SHROPSHIRE LAD II

Loveliest of trees, the cherry now
Is hung with bloom along the bough,
And stands about the woodland ride
Wearing white for Eastertide.

Now, of my threescore years and ten,
Twenty will not come again,
And take from seventy springs a score,
It only leaves me fifty more.

And since to look at things in bloom
Fifty springs are little room,
About the woodlands I will go
To see the cherry hung with snow.

A SHROPSHIRE LAD   XXVII

'Is my team ploughing,
　　That I was used to drive
And hear the harness jingle
　　When I was man alive?'

Ay, the horses trample,
　　The harness jingles now;
No change though you lie under
　　The land you used to plough.

'Is football playing
　　Along the river shore,
With lads to chase the leather,
　　Now I stand up no more?'

Ay, the ball is flying,
　　The lads play heart and soul;
The goal stands up, the keeper
　　Stands up to keep the goal.

'Is my girl happy,
   That I thought hard to leave,
And has she tired of weeping
   As she lies down at eve?'

Ay, she lies down lightly,
   She lies not down to weep:
Your girl is well contented,
   Be still, my lad and sleep.

'Is my friend hearty,
   Now I am thin and pine,
And has he found to sleep in
   A better bed than mine?'

Yes, lad, I lie easy,
   I lie as lads would choose;
I cheer a dead man's sweetheart,
   Never ask me whose.

A SHROPSHIRE LAD XXIII

The lads in their hundreds to Ludlow come in for the fair,
    There's men from the barn and the forge and the mill and
        the fold,
The lads for the girls and the lads for the liquor are there,
    And there with the rest are the lads that will never be old.

There's chaps from the town and the field and the till and the cart,
    And many to count are the stalwart, and many the brave,
And many the handsome of face and the handsome of heart,
    And few that will carry their looks or their truth to the grave.

I wish one could know them, I wish there were tokens to tell
    The fortunate fellows that now you can never discern;
And then one could talk with them friendly and wish them
        farewell
    And watch them depart on the way that they will not return.

But now you may stare as you like and there's nothing to scan;
    And brushing your elbow unguessed-at and not to be told
They carry back bright to the coiner the mintage of man,
    The lads that will die in their glory and never be old.

A SHROPSHIRE LAD XXXI

On Wenlock Edge the wood's in trouble;
    His forest fleece the Wrekin heaves;
The gale, it plies the saplings double,
    And thick on Severn snow the leaves.

'Twould blow like this through holt and hanger
    When Uricon the city stood:
'Tis the old wind in the old anger,
    But then it threshed another wood.

Then, 'twas before my time, the Roman
    At yonder heaving hill would stare:
The blood that warms an English yeoman,
    The thoughts that hurt him, they were there.

There, like the winds through woods in riot,
    Through him the gale of life blew high;
The tree of man was never quiet:
    Then 'twas the Roman, now 'tis I.

The gale, it plies the saplings double,
    It blows so hard, 'twill soon be gone:
To-day the Roman and his trouble
    Are ashes under Uricon.

A SHROPSHIRE LAD XXXII

From far, from eve and morning
    And yon twelve-winded sky,
The stuff of life to knit me
    Blew hither: here am I.

Now– for a breath I tarry
    Nor yet disperse apart –
Take my hand quick and tell me,
    What have you in your heart.

Speak now, and I will answer;
    How shall I help you, say;
Ere to the wind's twelve quarters
    I take my endless way.

A SHROPSHIRE LAD XXXV

On the idle hill of summer,
    Sleepy with the flow of streams,
Far I hear the steady drummer
    Drumming like a noise in dreams.

Far and near and low and louder
    On the roads of earth go by,
Dear to friends and food for powder,
    Soldiers marching, all to die.

East and west on fields forgotten
    Bleach the bones of comrades slain,
Lovely lads and dead and rotten;
    None that go return again.

Far the calling bugles hollo,
    High the screaming fife replies,
Gay the files of scarlet follow:
    Woman bore me, I will rise.

A SHROPSHIRE LAD XL

Into my heart an air that kills
   From yon far country blows:
What are those blue remembered hills,
   What spires, what farms are those?

That is the land of lost content,
   I see it shining plain,
The happy highways where I went
   And cannot come again.

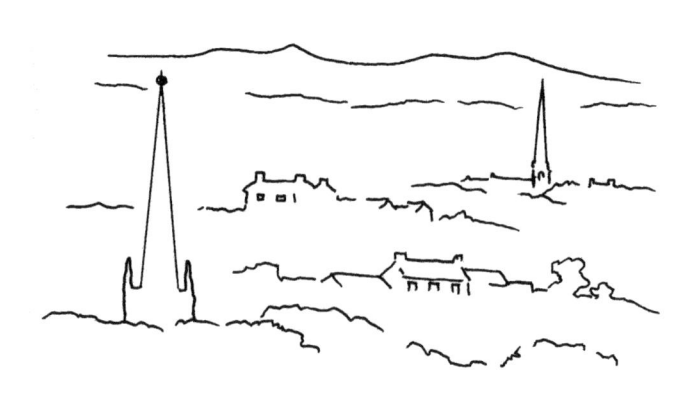

A SHROPSHIRE LAD LII

Far in a western brookland
  That bred me long ago
The poplars stand and tremble
  By pools I used to know.

There, in the windless night-time,
  The wanderer, marvelling why,
Halts on the bridge to hearken
  How soft the poplars sigh.

He hears: no more remembered
  In fields where I was known,
Here I lie down in London
  And turn to rest alone.

There, by the starlit fences,
  The wanderer halts and hears
My soul that lingers sighing
  About the glimmering weirs.

LAST POEMS XXXIX

When summer's end is nighing
    And skies at evening cloud,
I muse on change and fortune
    And all the feats I vowed
    When I was young and proud.

The weathercock at sunset
    Would lose the slanted ray,
And I would climb the beacon
    That looked to Wales away
    And saw the last of day.

From hill and cloud and heaven
    The hues of evening died;
Night welled through lane and hollow
    And hushed the countryside,
    But I had youth and pride.

And I with earth and nightfall
   In converse high would stand,
Late, till the west was ashen
   And darkness hard at hand,
   And the eye lost the land.

The year might age, and cloudy
   The lessening day might close,
But the air of other summers
   Breathed from beyond the snows,
   And I had hope of those.

They came and were and are not
   And come no more anew;
And all the years and seasons
   That ever can ensue
   Must now be worse and few.

So here's an end of roaming
   On eves when autumn nighs:
The ear too fondly listens
   For summer's parting sighs,
   And then the heart replies.

MORE POEMS XXIII

Crossing alone the nighted ferry
    With the one coin for fee,
Whom, on the wharf of Lethe waiting,
    Count you to find? Not me.

The brisk fond lackey to fetch and carry,
    The true, sick-hearted slave,
Expect him not in the just city
    And free land of the grave.

MORE POEMS XXXI

Because I liked you better
    Than suits a man to say,
It irked you, and I promised
    To throw the thought away.

To put the world between us
    We parted, stiff and dry;
'Good-bye,' said you, 'forget me.'
    'I will, no fear', said I.

If here, where clover whitens
    The dead man's knoll, you pass,
And no tall flower to meet you
    Starts in the trefoiled grass,

Halt by the headstone naming
    The heart no longer stirred,
And say the lad that loved you
    Was one that kept his word.

MORE POEMS XLVII

O thou that from thy mansion,
 Through time and place to roam,
Dost send abroad thy children,
 And then dost call them home,

That men and tribes and nations
 And all thy hand hath made
May shelter them from sunshine
 In thine eternal shade.

We now to peace and darkness
 And earth and thee restore
Thy creature that thou madest
 And wilt cast forth no more.

ADDITIONAL POEMS IX

When the bells justle in the tower
 The hollow night amid,
Then on my tongue the taste is sour
 Of all I ever did.

THE HOUSMAN SOCIETY

The Housman Society was founded in 1973. It exists primarily to promote knowledge and appreciation of the lives and works of A. E. Housman and other members of the family.

To this end it publishes an Annual Journal and regular newsletters and it has published a number of books about A. E. Housman. It celebrates the poet with commemorations in Bromsgrove and Ludlow. It organises an annual programme of events, including poetry readings, talks, discussions and visits to places associated with the family.

It also promotes the cause of literature and poetry in general. From 1996 to 2001 it organised major national poetry competitions and since 1998 it has sponsored annual lectures at the Hay Literary Festival by prominent people in the world of literature on *The Name and Nature of Poetry*. This title echoes that of a famous lecture given in 1933 by A. E. Housman in which he gave his view of what poetry was about.

For further information contact The Housman Society, 80 New Road, Bromsgrove, Worcestershire, B60 2LA.

The following poems and extracts from Geoffrey Hill's poems are reproduced by permission of Penguin Books Ltd. Extracts and cuts are made with the authority of the author.
From *Geoffrey Hill Collected Poems*, Penguin Books, London, 1985: Mercian Hymns, No. I (page 105), No. XIV (page 118), No. XXI (page 125), No. XXII (page 126) and XXV (page 129); *Tenebrae*, The Herefordshire Carol (page 164).
From *Canaan*, Penguin Books, London,1996: Sorrel (page 40), Pisgah (page 52), Mysticism and Democracy, Part One (page 55), and Of Constancy and Measure (page 68).
From The *Triumph of Love*, Penguin Books, London, 1999: No. VII (pages 2-3), No. LIII (pages 26-27), No. LXXXII (page 42), No. CVII (page 55), and No. CXXXVII (page 74).
From *The Orchards of Syon*, Penguin Books, London, 2002: No. XXII (page 22) line 5 to end, No. XXXVIII (page 38) line 5 to end, No. XLVIII (page 48) line 13 to end, No. LIV (page 54) line 13 to end, and No. LV (page 55).
From *A Treatise of Civil Power*, Penguin Books, London, 2007: A Cloud in Aquila (page 20).

Molly Holden's poems were first published as follows:
From *A Hill like a Horse*, Privately published, 1963: Worcestershire Lanes
From *To Make Me Grieve*, Chatto and Windus with The Hogarth Press, 1968: Dodderhill Woods, Photograph of Haymaker 1890, Teens, Birthplace, New-born.
From *Air and Chill Earth*, Chatto and Windus, 1971: Button Oak to Arley, Housman Country, After the Requested Cremation, Illness, Generations.
All of the above were reprinted in *New and Selected Poems*, Carcanet 1981, together with Of 1959.
None of these are currently in print.